Danny, King
of the Basement

David S. Craig

Playwrights Canada Press
Toronto • Canada

Playwrights Canada Press
215 Spadina Avenue, Suite 230, Toronto, Ontario CANADA M5T 2C7
416-703-0013
orders@playwrightscanada.com • www.playwrightscanada.com

Playwrights Canada Press acknowledges the support of
the taxpayers of Canada and the province of Ontario through
The Canada Council for the Arts and the Ontario Arts Council.

Cover photos of Gil Garratt and Yanna McIntosh by Tom Sandler.
Cover design & production editing: JLArt

Library and Archives Canada Cataloguing in Publication

Craig, David S. (David Stewart)
        Danny, king of the basement / David S. Craig.

A play.
ISBN 0-88754-726-5

        I. Title.

PS8555.R265D35 2004   C812'.54   C2004-903993-8

First edition: July 2004.
Printed and bound by Printco at Toronto, Canada.

*This play is dedicated to all the
mothers and children at Robertson House.
May they all find homes – safe and warm and soon.*

INTRODUCTION

David S. Craig's *Danny, King of the Basement* is an extraordinary play! It could wrongly be perceived as another "play with a message," the bane of the purist for whom drama has its own justification and its own delights and needs never to seek to change a flawed social order. But the most casual reading of this work reveals much more than a warning about the serious implications of child poverty on the quality of our society. Rather, one finds a moving story of an extraordinarily creative and imaginative boy named Danny who just happens to be poor. A boy that despite, or perhaps because of, having to move eight times in two years has developed a highly portable and admirable skill. The ability to make friends fast. When he moves onto middle class Clinton Street, Danny becomes the peacemaker between two warring neighbours. The result is a community with a "fun and games" constitution. A community that hears all, includes everyone and can heal even the most tenacious "brain freeze."

However, it scarcely needs saying that child poverty is the most pervasive embarrassment that faces Canada and the United States, nations who hold the dubious record of being the worst examples of this scourge in all the western world. In Canada, the House of Commons passed a resolution in 1988 promising "the elimination of child poverty" by the year 2000. By the coming of the new century and millennium, there were three times as many children in poverty as when the above resolution was recorded.

Magically, *Danny, King of the Basement* identifies virtually every disadvantage that social workers have outlined as the major hurdles placed in the path of the poor child—from constantly changing shelter arrangements in different neighbourhoods, to a continuing adjustment to new classes and teachers, to the lack of appropriate clothing for both work and play, to the constant need to find new companionship among a changing spectrum of peers—every challenge demanding a creative response that in some cases could not succeed. Danny is a marvelous combination of intelligence, energy, good-will and humour but eventually his disadvantages tragically threaten to bring him down. Humiliated by his inability to read, Danny faces a crisis he is totally unprepared for – not losing a home, but gaining one.

The characters that drive this story are priceless treasures in a cruel world. Their contrasting reactions to the challenges they face create a drama of rich depth and meaning. It is a play that moves the adult to tears and brings deep understanding to the young about the society they inhabit without ever humiliating the real poor kids that may be sitting in the audience. The play creates an opportunity for transformation that is quite unique.

The publication of *Danny, King of the Basement* creates, through the theatrical imagination, an opportunity to examine and understand the life of those at the bottom of the slippery ladder that we have built to discourage and frustrate a significant portion of our citizenry. I invite you to read, to laugh and to act.

—Walter Pitman

Walter Pitman's long career has included serving as Director of the Ontario Institute for Studies in Education, president of Ryerson Polytechnical and Dean of Arts and Science at Trent University. He was Executive Director of the Ontario Arts Council and NDP MP and MPP for Peterborough.

PLAYWRIGHT'S NOTES

I was inspired to write this play while driving my car. I say "inspired" because it's what I've heard writers say about the moment of beginning. For me the effect was more akin to grabbing a live wire. I was casually listening, as I always do, to CBC radio. They were talking about something called the Golden Report. The statistic that jolted me was this – 25% of homeless people in Toronto are children under the age of 12. I knew we had a problem with homelessness. I had no idea it affected so many kids. I knew I needed to do something as a parent of two children, as a citizen of Toronto and especially as a theatre artist. That knowing sustained me for the next four years of research, writing to opening.

I have three sincere and heartfelt thank you's. My old friend and colleague Richard Greenblatt who acted as dramaturge and director for this production. His enthusiasm, generous talent and deep commitment to this project, and theatre for young audiences in general, contributed enormously to the success of this play. To the Laidlaw Foundation, whose financial support of new artistic creation and its role in young lives was an important resource in the early days of development. And finally, to Tim Jennings, the Managing Director of Roseneath Theatre, who provided the practical framework without which theatre art cannot exist.

—David S. Craig
Toronto, 2004

Danny, King of the Basement premiered at the Lorraine Kimsa Theatre for Young People, Toronto, produced by Roseneath Theatre, in November 2001 with the following company:

LOUISE	Jennifer Dean
DANNY	Gil Garratt
PENELOPE	Yanna McIntosh
ANGELO	Ron Gabriel

Playwright/Producer	David S. Craig
Director/Dramaturge	Richard Greenblatt
Production Designer	Anjelija Djuric
Composer	Richard M. Sacks
Lighting Designer	Christina Cicko
Stage Manager	Kathryn Westoll
Study Guide	Pat McCarthy and Paula Owolabi

Danny, King of the Basement was commissioned with support from the Laidlaw Foundation and developed with a grant from the Canada Council of the Arts Creation Program.

In June of 2002, *Danny, King of the Basement* was awarded the Dora Mavor Moore Award for Outstanding Production – Theatre For Young Audiences, the Dora for Best Actor (TYA) Gil Garrett, and the Canada Council of the Arts Prize for TYA.

In June of 2004, the German translation of *Danny, King of the Basement* (*Agent im Spiel*, translated by Anke Ehlers) was nominated for the Deutscher Kindertheaterpreis Award in Frankfurt, Germany.

This published version is the seventy-minute play script that was performed at the premiere. Subsequent productions have used a fifty-two-minute touring version which can be purchased through Roseneath Theatre (info@roseneath.ca).

CHARACTERS

Principal Roles:
(in order of appearance)
LOUISE
DANNY
PENELOPE
ANGELO

Functionary Roles:
BILL*
STREETCAR DRIVER
ANGELO'S MOM
PENELOPE'S MOTHER
TAXI DRIVER
ANGELO'S DINOSAUR DAD*
ANGELO'S DAD*
PRINCIPAL*
RADIO BROADCASTER*
NURSE**
DOCTOR**

The functionary roles marked with an asterix* were all offstage voices which were taped. The nurse and the doctor (**) were played by the actors playing Angelo and Penelope. In this case, the actors concealed themselves in white gowns, hats and surgical masks. The other roles were played by actors playing the principal roles, as practical, who carried through two dimensional cartoon cut-outs or puppets. This maintained the integrity of the principal characters as three dimensional characters and added to the theatricality of the production.

This play was set in Toronto, and all the place names refer to real locations in that city. This was to emphasise to Toronto audiences that Danny's story was real and current. Producers mounting this production in other centres can apply to the playwright or his agents for permission to alter these references so that audiences in their community can have the same experience.

Danny, King of the Basement

PROLOGUE

Toronto. The present. A Thursday before dawn in late autumn.

Offstage, a man snores loudly. LOUISE enters cautiously, pulling a large suitcase.

LOUISE	*(whispering)* Danny… Danny… Danny!
DANNY	*(sleepy head appears)* Huh?
LOUISE	It's time.
DANNY	Huh?
LOUISE	Moving time.
DANNY	Why?
LOUISE	Because.
DANNY	Why because?
LOUISE	Because I say because.
DANNY	*(whining)* It's too early.
LOUISE	Danny – we have to go now. I don't want to wake Bill.
DANNY	Why?
LOUISE	Because I'm not saying goodbye.
DANNY	Why?
LOUISE	Because he didn't turn out to be Prince Charming did he?
DANNY	No.
LOUISE	So let's go.
DANNY	I gotta pack.

He disappears.

LOUISE	Make it fast.
DANNY	*(off)* I can pack faster than it takes to change a light bulb.

LOUISE	Yeah, yeah.
DANNY	I can pack faster than it takes to tie a shoelace.
LOUISE	Okay, okay.
DANNY	Faster than it take to–
LOUISE	Danny. Hurry up. If he wakes up–
DANNY	All ready.

He reappears with a shopping cart stuffed with found objects.

LOUISE	You can't take all that.
DANNY	It's my stuff.
LOUISE	You can't take it.
DANNY	It's my stuff!

The snoring stops. They freeze. Beat. Snoring starts again.

I'm not leaving without my stuff.

LOUISE	Okay, okay.
DANNY	What are you worried about. He'll sleep through anything.

A chorus of alarm clocks, buzzers and radio broadcasts. The snoring stops.

BILL	*(off)* Hey! Louise!

DANNY and LOUISE look at each other and run, pulling/carrying their bags behind them. A Toronto streetcar ("St. Clair Eastbound") glides to a stop.

DANNY	Hey. Streetcar. C'mon Mom.
LOUISE	All right, all right… gimme a hand.
DRIVER	Hey. You can't bring all that stuff on.
DANNY	Why not?
DRIVER	It's rush hour.

LOUISE	That's perfect. We're in a rush. C'mon Danny. Excuse me. Could we have a little space in here?
	They squeeze on. Sounds of disgruntled passengers. Their faces appear in a window, LOUISE in front, DANNY behind. The streetcar bell rings and they move off.
DANNY	That was so fun.
LOUISE	I'm glad you think so.
DANNY	We made a clean getaway.
LOUISE	Yeah. I'm good at escaping.
DANNY	C'mon Mom. You love moving.
LOUISE	No. You love moving, and we move too much.
DANNY	I'm the King of Moving.
LOUISE	It's not good for you. It's been seven times in three years.
DANNY	Eight times in two years. But who's counting.
LOUISE	I'm counting. I was so sure that place was going to work out. So sure.
DANNY	Hey truck driver!
	DANNY mimes pulling a horn cord. The truck driver blows a big air horn.
LOUISE	Danny Carter get your hands in the window. You're getting your jacket all dirty.
DANNY	It's not a jacket, it's a super coat.
LOUISE	I wish.
DANNY	So where we going? The shelter? Let's go to Robertson House. They gotta big TV.
LOUISE	I've rented a basement apartment.
DANNY	Another basement?
LOUISE	This is a good one, Danny, first class, blue chip, solid gold. It's got no mould, no bugs, and a window you can actually see through.

DANNY	I hate basements.
LOUISE	You're gonna love this one. But first we're going to Human Resources.
DANNY	Why?!
LOUISE	To get a job, Mr. Banker. We're broke.
DANNY	You never get a job there.
LOUISE	I did once.
DANNY	When?
LOUISE	Okay, it was before you were born, but I did. Besides, today I feel lucky. How do we get there?
DANNY	Well, we could go streetcar to Yonge Street and then subway south to Summerhill, Rosedale, Bloor, Wellesley, College, Dundas, Queen and walk west. Or, we could go streetcar to St. Clair East and subway south to Davenport, Spadina, St. George, Museum, Queen's Park, St. Patrick, Osgoode, St. Andrew and walk east. Take your pick.
LOUISE	You're amazing.
DANNY	No, you're amazing.
LOUISE	No, you're amazing.
DANNY	Okay, I'm amazing.
LOUISE	I better call your school and tell them you're not coming back. Is there anyone you want to say goodbye to?
DANNY	No.
LOUISE	What about that boy Ahmed? You were friends with him, weren't you? *(beat)* Danny?
DANNY	Hey, truck driver.

> *DANNY mimes pulling a horn cord. The truck driver blows a big air horn.*
>
> *The streetcar moves off.*

ACT ONE

> *Clinton Street. Afternoon.*
>
> *There are steps up to PENELOPE's front door. There are steps down to the basement apartment. Beside PENELOPE's house, at ground level, is ANGELO's front door.*
>
> *Thunder sounds.*
>
> *ANGELO'S MOM enters from her first job. She opens her front door...*

ANGELO'S MOM   *(calling in)* Home.

> *...and exits. PENELOPE's MOTHER enters followed by PENELOPE.*

PENELOPE   Mom... Mom... Mother!

MOTHER   What?

PENELOPE   I want to talk to you.

MOTHER   Not now.

PENELOPE   But it's important.

MOTHER   Penelope, I've taken you to the shoe store, I've taken you to the coat store and today I took you to the hairdresser. But now, Mommy needs to be alone, and you're going to play outside.

PENELOPE   Play?

MOTHER   Yes.

PENELOPE   Here?

MOTHER   Yes.

PENELOPE   What about ballet?

MOTHER   I'll call you a taxi.

PENELOPE   But there's no one to play with.

MOTHER   What about Angelo? Play with Angelo.

PENELOPE   A boy? You want me to play with a boy?

MOTHER   It won't hurt you.

PENELOPE   Oh yes it will. Playing with a boy is torture. Playing with that boy is death.

MOTHER   Penelope, if you don't stay outside, I will cancel your ballet classes, I will cancel your acting classes and I will stuff all your movies into the Garburator. *(PENELOPE gasps.)* Have a nice play.

> *MOTHER exits. Door slams. PENELOPE pulls out a cell phone.*

PENELOPE   *(quickly)* Mom, please don't hang up, please don't hang up, pleeeeeeeease…. Thank you. I really want to go back to my old school…. I want to discuss it again…. Because my friends are all there…. Why can't we afford it anymore?… But he never… okay… okay… okay! *(She hangs up.)*

> *PENELOPE tries a number on her cell phone.*

Hi Daddy… it's me. Please call. It's really, really, really important. Love you.

> *ANGELO staggers in with a colossal hockey bag on his back. PENELOPE watches.*

You dropped something.

> *ANGELO awkwardly turns.*

It's over there.

ANGELO   Yeah right.

PENELOPE   It is. It is. I swear. It's right behind you. *(ANGELO looks. It's not there.)*

ANGELO   Thanks Penny.

PENELOPE   You're welcome.

ANGELO   Thanks for nothing.

PENELOPE   Did you score? *(ANGELO says nothing.)* You didn't did you. Ooooooo, your dad is going to get reeeeeeeeee-ly angry. He's going to yell and scream and blow a hole in your roof. And then you'll cry, boo-hoo, like you did the last time.

ANGELO drops his bag and suddenly comes towards PENELOPE who screams and runs up her stairs.

You can't come up here. It's private property. You can't, you can't, you CAAAAAAAAN'T!

ANGELO turns away in disgust.

Did you see my shoes? They're new.

ANGELO   Who cares.

PENELOPE   They cost two hundred dollars.

ANGELO   So what.

PENELOPE   And I got a new coat. And I got my hair done. In a real salon. Cost a hundred and forty dollars. *(ANGELO snorts.)* It did.

ANGELO   A hundred and forty bucks for that?

PENELOPE   It looks great.

ANGELO   Maybe for your old school.

PENELOPE   What do you know. You didn't even notice.

ANGELO   Oh yes I did. I noticed right away. I just didn't want to show how much I was laughing but now that I know it cost a hundred and forty bucks I just have to tell you. Your hair sucks.

PENELOPE   Shut up, Angelo.

A taxi roars up and squeals to a halt.

ANGELO   Ooooh, a taxi. Going back to the hair butcher? Good idea 'cause everyone at school is going to laugh.

PENELOPE   Yeah well at least I'm popular. At least I've got friends. At least I'm not a loser.

DRIVER   Where to?

PENELOPE   Pia Bauman Dance Studio, *s'il vous plait.* Bye loser.

PENELOPE drives off.

ANGELO   (*shouting after*) I'm not a loser. I scored a goal. (*to
                himself*) Almost.

                ANGELO shoulders his bag and opens his front door.

                (*fearfully*) Dad? Dad?

                *A dinosaur roars. A dinosaur shadow appears in the
                window.*

                I'm home.

                ANGELO exits.

                *DANNY enters at a run with his knapsack, pushing
                his shopping cart. He crosses the stage and suddenly
                slams on the brakes. He backs up to 92, runs down
                the stairs to check the basement door. It's locked.*

                ANGELO'S MOM enters. DANNY hides.

ANGELO'S
MOM   Ciao.

                ANGELO'S MOM exits to her second job.

                *DANNY returns to his cart. He pulls out a
                microphone.*

DANNY   Game agent D. Delco on site at 92B for basement Clinton
                Street. Visual contact confirmed but door locked, repeat
                door locked. Request hyperlink for key, repeat, need key
                now.

LOUISE   (*off*) Danny, I've got the key.

DANNY   Wow. Nice response, time control. Delco out.

                *Dinosaur roar. ANGELO comes out with a bag of
                garbage. DANNY hides.*

ANGELO   Okay, okay.

                Dinosaur roars.

                I said I'll do it. Sheesh.

                *ANGELO drops the bag in a garbage can, but then
                notices DANNY's cart and bag. He walks over to it
                and picks up the microphone.*

Hello? Hello? *(He checks to make sure he's alone.)* I'd like a large pizza with double pepperoni and–

DANNY   Hey.

ANGELO   Huh?

DANNY   Are you an agent?

ANGELO   What?

DANNY   A game agent.

ANGELO   No.

DANNY   But you were using the uplink.

ANGELO   I was pretending.

DANNY   I knew it.

ANGELO   I didn't know it was yours.

DANNY   This is game property. Comes from everywhere. Belongs to everyone. What's your disguise?

ANGELO   Disguise?

DANNY   Yeah. Game agents always have disguises.

LOUISE   *(off)* Danny!?

DANNY   Over here. See that woman?

ANGELO   Yeah.

DANNY   She's a game agent disguised as my mother. Watch.

LOUISE enters, pulling a huge rolling suitcase.

LOUISE   Please tell me we're here.

DANNY   We're here.

LOUISE   Finally. My dogs are so sore they're barking. This bag has a broken wheel, curse my Irish luck, not that I'm Irish. We're both bagged. The bag and I. Both bagged. Aw, never mind. Hi. I'm Louise. I'm Danny's mother.

DANNY   Good disguise, eh?

ANGELO   I got to go.

LOUISE	Hold on a sec.
ANGELO	I really gotta go.
LOUISE	You didn't tell me your name. I told you my name.
ANGELO	I'm Angelo.
LOUISE	Angelo. Pleased to meet'cha. We're moving into 92B. Maybe Danny can walk to school with you tomorrow.
ANGELO	There is no school tomorrow.
LOUISE	No school?
ANGELO	It's a P.A. day. Bye.
LOUISE	Bye. Oh. Angelo. Is there a breakfast program at your school?
ANGELO	A what?
LOUISE	A thing for kids who need breakfast.
ANGELO	I dunno. Bye.

ANGELO exits.

LOUISE	He seems like a nice boy.
DANNY	Don't ask him that.
LOUISE	Ask him what?
DANNY	If there's a breakfast program.
LOUISE	Why not?
DANNY	It'll blow my cover.
LOUISE	Did you tell him I was disguised as your mother?
DANNY	Maybe.
LOUISE	Danny. I'm not a saint but I am your mother.
DANNY	You got any food?
LOUISE	Not a turnip. You hungry again?
DANNY	Yeah but who's counting.
LOUISE	I'm counting. Lets put the bags inside and go to the store.

As she speaks, she moves the bags inside.

DANNY   You go and I'll watch the bags.

LOUISE   It'll just take a second. Don't you want to see inside?

DANNY   I'll wait out here.

LOUISE   Just take a peek.

DANNY   Mom, I'm starving.

LOUISE   All right, all right. We'll have our first meal in our new home. What'll it be? Chicken? Steak?

DANNY   Yeah right. How about salami.

LOUISE   Okay, and eggs and cheese and bread–

DANNY   We've got seven bucks.

LOUISE   Seven?

DANNY   We had to take the TTC twice and you didn't get a job.

LOUISE   I dunno what happened. I was feeling so lucky.

DANNY   Just get salami and eggs.

LOUISE   How about cheese instead of eggs.

DANNY   Eggs are cheaper. What about potatoes?

LOUISE   Baked potatoes and butter.

DANNY   Butter costs like three bucks.

LOUISE   I've got some butter packets in my purse.

DANNY   Okay. Salami, eggs, potatoes and if there's money left over ice cream.

LOUISE   Danny, do I look like a dough head. If there's money left over I'm buying carrots.

DANNY   Mom…

LOUISE   And you're going to eat them. *(hand out)* Let's have the money, Mr. Banker.

    DANNY carefully counts out six dollars and eighty-six cents from his purse.

DANNY	That's all we have.
LOUISE	I know.
DANNY	Go straight there and back.
LOUISE	I will.
DANNY	No cigarettes.
LOUISE	No cigarettes.
DANNY	Go straight there and back, okay?
LOUISE	Look, Danny… I know I've let you down but this time I promise it's going to be different. And I know I've promised that before too, but this time I mean it. This time its going to work out just the way we dreamed.
DANNY	With Dad?
LOUISE	Not with your dad, with us. Right here. 92B for basement. *(DANNY looks at his feet.)* Here's the key. Go in if you get cold, okay?
DANNY	I won't go in 'til you get back.
LOUISE	*(going off)* But go in if you're cold, okay?
DANNY	*(calling)* I won't go in 'til you get back.
LOUISE	*(off)* Go in if you get cold.

> *LOUISE exits. DANNY runs to his cart.*

DANNY	This is Agent D. Delco working undercover deep in alien territory. I need back-up, repeat, need back-up now…. Control, say something. Please. You've got to hear me. This is a code red. I'm losing power. I can't hold on. *(gasps for air)* Need… back-up… now.

> *DANNY collapses. ANGELO walks out his door with a hockey stick. He approaches DANNY cautiously.*

DANNY	*(to ANGELO)* Hi! Thanks Control. Back-up has arrived. Delco out.
ANGELO	Who are you talking to?
DANNY	Control. Wanna play?

ANGELO	No.
	ANGELO shoots with his hockey stick. DANNY watches.
ANGELO	She's your real mother, isn't she?
DANNY	Who?
ANGELO	That lady who was here. She's not a part of any game. She's your real mother.
DANNY	It's probably safer for you to think that.
ANGELO	Why?
DANNY	In case you're tortured.
ANGELO	Tortured?
DANNY	Never mind. I'll tell ya later. Right now I need another agent. Someone who knows what's going on around here.
ANGELO	I know what's going on.
DANNY	What?
ANGELO	Nothing.
DANNY	There's always something going on. Surprise attacks, escapes, missions…
ANGELO	You're makin' this up, aren't you.
DANNY	Yeah. Fun, eh?
	A taxi roars in and screeches to a halt. PENELOPE gets out. The taxi roars off.
PENELOPE	Andjee. Are you still alive? I guess you were too scared to tell your father you didn't score. I guess that's why he didn't bite your head off. Too bad you can't be like me. Madam says I have a perfect turn out. Have a nice time being a loser.
	She exits and slams the door.
DANNY	Whoah. Sneak attack or what. *(ANGELO turns away.)* Who was that?
ANGELO	The meanest person in the universe.

DANNY	What's her name?
ANGELO	Penny the whiner.
DANNY	What's her disguise?
ANGELO	Godzilla the Hut.
DANNY	Could you tell me about her?
ANGELO	Oh yeah. I could tell you a lot about her.
DANNY	That's what a game agent does. Reports, gathers information, hangs out. But I guess you wanna play hockey.
ANGELO	Wait. If she's out, I'm in.
DANNY	Yeah?
ANGELO	Totally.
DANNY	Then you're in.
ANGELO	Yes. I'm in and sheeeeeeee's OUT! What do I do?
DANNY	So what's your disguise?
ANGELO	I dunno.
DANNY	You gotta have one. I've got hundreds.
ANGELO	Why?
DANNY	For protection. Who do you want to be?
ANGELO	I want to be number 13 – Mats Sundin.
DANNY	Okay.
ANGELO	No. I wanna be Jackie Chan.
DANNY	Okay.
ANGELO	But no one would believe it.
DANNY	Yeah. *(idea)* I know. You could be disguised as my best friend.
ANGELO	What?
DANNY	It's perfect. We live on the same street, we go to the same school–

ANGELO	Yeah but you just moved in. No one makes a best friend that fast.
DANNY	Oh yeah? I can make a friend in a morning and a best friend in a day.
ANGELO	You're kidding.
DANNY	I'm serious.
ANGELO	For real?
DANNY	Totally.

ANGELO laughs.

ANGELO	Okay. I'm in disguise. What do we do now?
DANNY	I dunno.
ANGELO	Let's hang out.
DANNY	Cool.

DANNY hands out sunglasses and they hang out.

ANGELO	This is so great. Before you came there was no one to be with except Penelope. But you got to call her Penny 'cause she hates that.

Dinosaur roars.

DANNY	What was that?
ANGELO	What?
DANNY	That noise. It came from your house.
ANGELO	Oh. Uh. That's my dad.
DANNY	Your dad? But he sounds like a dinosaur.
ANGELO	Yeah.

Dinosaur roars.

I gotta go.

DANNY	Go for dinner?
ANGELO	Yeah.
DANNY	What are you having?

ANGELO	Meatballs.
DANNY	Nice.
ANGELO	Not. He makes it every night.
DANNY	With spaghetti?
ANGELO	Yeah.
DANNY	And tomato sauce?
ANGELO	Yeah.
DANNY	Really nice.

DANNY drifts away.

ANGELO	Hey. See you later "buddy."
DANNY	Okay, "pal."

ANGELO exits. Time passes. DANNY is cold. He stomps his feet and flaps his hands.

PENELOPE enters with a garbage bag.

PENELOPE	Excuse me.
DANNY	Yeah?
PENELOPE	Is this your stuff?
DANNY	Yeah.
PENELOPE	Well excuse me it's on private property.
DANNY	I know.
PENELOPE	This is my house.
DANNY	I know.
PENELOPE	So. Like. Leave.
DANNY	I can't. I live here.
PENELOPE	Where?
DANNY	There.
PENELOPE	In my house?
DANNY	Yeah.

PENELOPE	How can you live in my house?
DANNY	I'm a game agent. I live everywhere. I'm in disguise.
PENELOPE	No you're not. You're one of Angelo's stupid little friends.
DANNY	*(surprised)* How did you know we were friends?
PENELOPE	Cause you're stupid like he is. You think it's so cool to walk around without a coat on.
DANNY	I have a coat; you just can't see it. It's a super coat.
PENELOPE	A what?
DANNY	It's a coat that shoots hot air out the arms so your hands never get cold and shoots hot air down onto the sidewalk so the ice melts and you never fall down and it shoots hot air right up into the air so the snow melts and you don't even need a hat.
PENELOPE	As if.
DANNY	It's true. You should get one.
PENELOPE	I like this coat. You know how much it cost? A lot.
DANNY	You know how much my super coat cost? Nothing.
PENELOPE	Cause you made it up.
DANNY	Right and I can make up anything I want which means I can have anything I want.
	PENELOPE has to admit she's impressed.
PENELOPE	Where do you live really?
DANNY	In that house.
PENELOPE	You can't. That's where I live.
DANNY	So do I.
PENELOPE	You do not.
DANNY	Do so.
PENELOPE	Wanna bet?
DANNY	You'd lose.
PENELOPE	No.

DANNY	Yes.
PENELOPE	No.
DANNY	Yes.
PENELOPE	I'll bet you anything you don't live in that house.
DANNY	I don't wanna bet.
PENELOPE	'Cause you're lying.
DANNY	I don't lie.
PENELOPE	Then bet.
DANNY	Okay. I bet my super coat against your new coat.
PENELOPE	Your coat is made up.
DANNY	Yeah but I know I'm going to win so I'll risk it.
PENELOPE	It's a deal. If you live in my house, which you don't, you can have my new coat. But if you don't live in my house, I get your super coat and you have to be my slave for life.
DANNY	Are you sure you want to do this?
PENELOPE	Yes.
DANNY	Cause I absolutely do live in your house.
PENELOPE	That house.
DANNY	Yeah.
PENELOPE	That house right there.
DANNY	Yeah.
PENELOPE	Prove it.
DANNY	I live in the basement. Here's the key. 92B for basement Clinton Street.
PENELOPE	AAAAAAAAAAAAAAAAAAAAAARGH!!!
DANNY	Can I have my coat?
PENELOPE	You can't live there. My mother rented the basement to a single woman.
DANNY	Yeah, well, so, the single women has a kid.

PENELOPE	But you don't live in my home. You live in your home.
DANNY	Yeah but my home is in that house. Coat please.
PENELOPE	No. I just got it today. What will I tell my mother?
DANNY	Tell her the truth.
PENELOPE	I can't tell her that.
DANNY	Okay. I'll tell her.
PENELOPE	No! You don't understand. She'll get so mad. She'll blow up the whole block. She'll blow up the whole city. There'll be nothing left but a huge smoking hole in the ground.
DANNY	Aw. Coat please.
PENELOPE	Look. I'm sorry I made the stupid bet. I'll do anything to get out of it.
DANNY	Anything?
PENELOPE	Anything.
DANNY	How can I trust you?
PENELOPE	I'll swear.
DANNY	Okay. Swear on the thing you want most in your life.
PENELOPE	I want to be a movie star.
DANNY	Not in your dreams. In your life.
PENELOPE	I dunno.
DANNY	You don't know what you want most in your life?
PENELOPE	Well what if I do? I'm sure not going to tell some kid on the street I've never even met before.
DANNY	You gotta tell. You gotta tell everyone so it'll come true. I wanna be with my dad. He lives in the Rocky Mountains, fighting fires. More than anything else I want to live in the mountains with my mom and dad.
PENELOPE	I want my parents to talk to each other.
DANNY	That's all?

PENELOPE	My dad moved out and I don't know why and I really want them to tell me what's going on and… and…
DANNY	Talk to each other.
PENELOPE	Yeah. That's what I want more than anything else in the world.
DANNY	Okay. Swear on that and you can have your coat back.
PENELOPE	That's all?
DANNY	And be nice to my friends.
PENELOPE	I swear.

DANNY returns her coat.

That was so easy.

DANNY	Yeah but don't forget.
PENELOPE	I won't.
MOTHER	*(off)* Penelope.
PENELOPE	Coming. Hey. What's your name?
DANNY	Danny Carter.
MOTHER	Penelope. Dinner.
PENELOPE	I'M COMING!!! I gotta go in.
DANNY	What are you having?
PENELOPE	I dunno. Steak, fries, Caesar salad.
DANNY	Nice.
PENELOPE	Are you cold?
DANNY	Do I look cold?
PENELOPE	Yeah.
DANNY	It's a disguise.
PENELOPE	Oh…
DANNY	Fun, eh?
PENELOPE	Yeah. See ya.

> *PENELOPE exits. Again DANNY is cold but now he is having trouble concealing it.*
>
> *LOUISE enters. She sees DANNY before he sees her.*

LOUISE Danny! Have you been waiting outside all this time?

DANNY Where were you?

LOUISE At the store.

DANNY You were supposed to come straight back.

LOUISE Well excuse me, something happened.

DANNY *(accusing)* Cigarettes?

LOUISE No.

DANNY Breathe.

LOUISE *(She does.)* See. I said I quit and I meant it.

DANNY What took you so long?

LOUISE I'll tell you if you lay off a second. Cripes, you sound like a case worker.

DANNY Well... where were you?

LOUISE C'mon in and I'll tell you about it.

DANNY No. Tell me now.

LOUISE Danny–

DANNY Tell me here.

LOUISE Okay, okay, I'll tell you but I gotta sit down. And you gotta sit next to me. Holy Hannah, you're freezing. *(She wraps her coat around him.)*

DANNY What happened?

LOUISE Okay, okay – I was walking home from the Super Save when I pass this sandwich shop and I see a sign in the window that says, "Waitress Wanted." Now am I a waitress anymore?

DANNY No.

LOUISE Right. I'm a...

DANNY	…Government-trained web page designer.
LOUISE	But then I think, "Louise, you've just spent your last dime on a potato. Beggars can't be choosers."
DANNY	We're not beggars.
LOUISE	You're right. We're millionaires with no money. But just the same, in spite of being millionaires, I go back and meet the owner—Joe's his name – Old Joe's his disguise— and I let him know he's speaking with–
DANNY	Somebody to be reckoned with.
LOUISE	And I do a little–
DANNY	Razzle-dazzle.
LOUISE	And he gives me the job! Well can we have a little excitement?
DANNY	Are you telling the truth?
LOUISE	Truth, Danny. True blue. And you know what it means? It means I can pay the rent. And if I can pay the rent we can stay. Stay for a long time.
DANNY	Like for three months?
LOUISE	Way longer than that.
DANNY	Yeah but you forgot one thing. The landlady thinks she rented the apartment to a single woman.
LOUISE	How do you know that?
DANNY	'Cause the landlady's daughter told me.
LOUISE	You make friends fast.
DANNY	Did you think you could hide me?
LOUISE	Do you know how hard it is for people like us to get an apartment, to find a place to live? If I told her about you she'd never have let us in.
DANNY	Well now she's going to kick us out.
LOUISE	No she won't, Danny, believe me. She's got her own problems.

DANNY	What problems?
LOUISE	Adult problems.
DANNY	What problems?
LOUISE	She needs the money.
DANNY	She's not broke. She's rich.
LOUISE	I know. But believe it or not, rich people can think they're broke. Danny believe me, this is our lucky break. A job I can walk to. A place of our own. Our moving days are over.
DANNY	I like moving.
LOUISE	Wait 'til you see this place. It's like a cozy little cave.

LOUISE exits.

DANNY	Is there cable?
LOUISE	*(off)* No.
DANNY	DVD?
LOUISE	*(off)* No.
DANNY	TV? Mom?

LOUISE re-enters.

LOUISE	You know what? Who needs it.
DANNY	No TV?!
LOUISE	It wasn't a priority.
DANNY	What am I gonna do without TV?!?!
LOUISE	*(firmly)* Homework.
DANNY	*(He gasps.)* Control it's Delco…
LOUISE	Home cooked meals…
DANNY	I got no air.
LOUISE	And for me, home at night.
DANNY	Beam me outta here. Got. No. Air.

LOUISE   Danny. Stand up and stop fooling around. You're going to
            get your clothes all dirty. Danny. Get up.

            He does so sullenly.

            Why are you being so difficult?

DANNY   Why are you being so mean?

LOUISE   I'm trying to be your mother.

DANNY   I thought we were friends.

LOUISE   Yeah? Well. The friend thing isn't working so good right
            now. From now on, I'm just going to be your mother.

DANNY   I don't want a mother.

LOUISE   Tough. You got one. Now inside. It's dinner, bath and bed
            for you, mister. Dinner, bath and bed.

            They exit. The moon comes out.

            ANGELO'S MOM enters…

ANGELO'S
MOM   Home.

            *…and exits. A raccoon gets into the garbage. The
            moon sets.*

ACT TWO

The next day.

A chorus of alarm clocks, buzzers and radio broadcasts. The sun comes up.

ANGELO'S MOM enters…

ANGELO'S MOM   Ciao.

…and exits.

A garbage truck drives on, picks up the garbage in front of ANGELO's house and PENELOPE's house and exits.

A taxi rushes on and screeches to a halt. PENELOPE's MOTHER rushes on and shouts back through the door.

MOTHER   Penelope. There's money for lunch on the counter, I'll be back by noon, don't watch too much TV.

The MOTHER jumps into the taxi and exits. As it leaves, PENELOPE enters.

PENELOPE   Mother!

PENELOPE dials a cell phone as she exits back into the house slamming the door.

Immediately there is the roar of a dinosaur and ANGELO rushes on. ANGELO timidly returns to the door.

ANGELO   Uh… Dad…?

There is another roar. A hockey stick sails out the door and into ANGELO's hands.

Thanks.

The dinosaur grumbles. ANGELO begins to practise.

LOUISE enters on her way to work.

LOUISE   Good morning, Angelo.

ANGELO   Hi.

LOUISE	How do I look?
ANGELO	Okay.
LOUISE	Just okay?
ANGELO	You look fine.
LOUISE	Thanks. It's my first day at a new job. Listen, can Danny hang out with you 'til I get back?
ANGELO	I guess so.
LOUISE	Great. Well. I'm off to work. See you after work. Wish me luck. At work!

> *LOUISE exits. ANGELO practises. PENELOPE enters.*

PENELOPE	What are you doing, Anjee?
ANGELO	None of your business.
PENELOPE	Practising?
ANGELO	Go away.
PENELOPE	It won't do any good.
ANGELO	Go away!
PENELOPE	Ooooh.
ANGELO	Look. Why don't you just ignore me like when you went to that private school.
PENELOPE	Who says I ever noticed you.

> *A cell phone rings. PENELOPE pulls one out of her pocket.*

Hello?

> *A cell phone continues to ring. PENELOPE pulls out another cell phone.*

Hello…. Hi Dad. *(turning away from ANGELO)* Where are you?… Yeah…. Yeah…. Did you get my message?… That's okay. I just really need to talk to you 'cause I really, really want to go back to my old school…. Because my friends are all there…. I asked Mom but she said to speak

to you…. Well because you haven't sent the check….
Okay, okay, don't get mad at me…. Okay…. Yeah….
Okay…. Yeah…. Okay…. Okay! I'll tell her.

She puts the phone away.

(to ANGELO) What?!

ANGELO	*Two* cell phones?
PENELOPE	So?
ANGELO	Why do you need *two* cell phones?
PENELOPE	Obviously because one is not enough.
ANGELO	Yeah, right.
PENELOPE	Because there are so many people wanting to call me.
ANGELO	Yeah right.
PENELOPE	So I just *have* to be available.
ANGELO	Yeah right.
PENELOPE	Is that all you can say?
ANGELO	Yeah r–. No.
PENELOPE	Uch. Why am I even talking to you?
ANGELO	Maybe 'cause your cell phones aren't ringing, Penny.
PENELOPE	Don't call me that.
ANGELO	'Cause no one wants to talk to you, Penny.
PENELOPE	I've got lots of friends.
ANGELO	You know what you get with a hundred Penny's? A Loony.
PENELOPE	Oh ha, ha, ha.

Cell phone rings.

Hello? *(wrong phone)* Shut up. Hello… *(flat)* Hi Mom…

ANGELO	*(taunting)* Ah-hah.
PENELOPE	SHUT UP!… No not you…. Yes, he called…. Yes I asked him about it…. He said the cheque is in the mail…. Of

course I believed him…. Mom, please don't…. Okay….
Okay…. Okay…

PENELOPE moves off. DANNY comes out of hiding.

DANNY	Pssssst.
ANGELO	Hi.
DANNY	Shhh.
ANGELO	Is this part of the game?
DANNY	Of course.
ANGELO	Great.
DANNY	Were you contacted?
ANGELO	Huh?
DANNY	Were you contacted?
PENELOPE	Okay. I'll tell him.
ANGELO	I don't think so.
DANNY	You have to be sure, you have to be positive.
ANGELO	I had breakfast with my dad.
PENELOPE	I'll tell him.
DANNY	Did she talk to you?
ANGELO	Yeah.
DANNY	So you were contacted.
ANGELO	Is she in this?
PENELOPE	I said I'll tell him!
DANNY	Everyone is.
ANGELO	Oh no. If she's in, I'm out.
DANNY	Why?
ANGELO	I told you. She's the meanest person in the universe.
DANNY	That's a disguise.
PENELOPE	I'll teeeeeelllll hiiiiiim!!!

PENELOPE hangs up.

ANGELO	With her it's permanent.
DANNY	Watch. *(to PENELOPE)* Hi.
PENELOPE	Hi. I told my mother about you.
DANNY	And?
PENELOPE	She was really mad.
DANNY	And?
PENELOPE	I convinced her to let you stay as long as you pay the rent.
DANNY	Did you tell her I was a game agent?
PENELOPE	No.
DANNY	Phew. For a second there I was worried. Wanna play?
PENELOPE	Play? Play what?
DANNY	I dunno. Hey Angelo, wha'd'ya wanna play?
PENELOPE	I'm not playing anything with him.
DANNY	Why not? He's your neighbour, isn't he?
PENELOPE	He's my neighbour unfortunately.
ANGELO	I'm gone.
DANNY	Wait. Penelope doesn't know you're my friend.
ANGELO	You think that's going to make a difference?
DANNY	Oh yeah I think it'll make a big difference. If she remembers what she promised.
PENELOPE	I didn't promise– Oh yeah.
DANNY	She remembers! So what'd'ya wanna play?
ANGELO	Me?
DANNY	Yeah.
ANGELO	With her?
DANNY	Yeah.
ANGELO	She hates my guts.

DANNY   Well, she really wants to play with you now. Don't you, Penny?

PENELOPE   *(through gritted teeth)* Yeah.

DANNY   See?

ANGELO   Okay. I wanna play hockey.

PENELOPE   No!

DANNY   Hockey sounds great. You got sticks?

ANGELO   Yeah.

>   *ANGELO runs to get hockey sticks.*

PENELOPE   Please don't make me play hockey.

DANNY   Why not?

PENELOPE   I hate hockey.

DANNY   Have you ever played?

PENELOPE   No.

DANNY   You might like it.

PENELOPE   I don't know the rules.

DANNY   We'll make them up.

PENELOPE   I hate making things up.

>   *ANGELO enters with shinny sticks and the wettest, grungiest, hairiest ball in the world.*

ANGELO   Okay. One on one.

DANNY   Okay. Yeah.

ANGELO   I'm Sundin. Yeah.

DANNY   Who am I?

ANGELO   You're Lemieux.

DANNY   Is he good?

ANGELO   Oh yeah.

PENELOPE   Who am I?

ANGELO	You drop the puck.
PENELOPE	Oh yay. Where is it?
ANGELO	Catch.
PENELOPE	Ew. Ew. Ew. Ew. Yuck!
DANNY & ANGELO	What?
PENELOPE	That is the most disgusting thing in the universe. Ew. I am not touching it again.

She wipes her hand on DANNY.

ANGELO	Aw, c'mon.
PENELOPE	Oh no. That thing is so full of germs it's alive.
ANGELO	How can we play without a puck?
DANNY	No problem. We can use a game puck.
ANGELO	What?
DANNY	A game puck. Here comes Lemieux. He's coming up to Sundin.
ANGELO	But Sundin intercepts, skates down the ice and scores.
DANNY	The crowd goes wild.
PENELOPE	And Penelope is bored.
ANGELO	Okay. Game pucks rule.
DANNY	You're fast.
ANGELO	Am I?
DANNY	Oh yeah.
ANGELO	You'd be fast too if it weren't for those boots.
PENELOPE	Your boots are so big.
DANNY	They're okay.
PENELOPE	They're pathetic.
ANGELO	Who cares. Let's play. Face off! To Sundin. He dekes past Lemieux. He's in the clear. But no. It's amazing.

	He's skating back. He's skating circles around Lemieux down the ice and scores.
PENELOPE	Excuse me. What am I supposed to do?
ANGELO	You cheer. For me.
DANNY	She can be the goalie.
PENELOPE	Okay, okay, so where's the net thingy?
ANGELO	There isn't one. It's a game net.
PENELOPE	Oh! *(to herself)* So I can do whatever I want.
	DANNY takes off his boots.
DANNY	News flash. Lemieux is changing into his super skates. He's ready to play.
ANGELO	In your socks?
DANNY	You got a problem?
PENELOPE	You'll freeze.
DANNY	In super skates? Wrong. I'll be fast. Face off! It's Lemieux, he's got the puck, he dekes past Sundin and–
PENELOPE	Scores.
ANGELO	He didn't even shoot.
PENELOPE	He still scores.
ANGELO	Okay. Face off. Sundin has the puck–
DANNY	Lemieux is after him–
ANGELO	Sundin breaks free, he shoots–
PENELOPE	But it goes… over there.
ANGELO	Aw…
DANNY	Which gives Lemieux a chance to shoot.
PENELOPE	And he scores. Tie game. The crowd goes wild.
ANGELO	Okay. The game is into overtime. Next goal wins. A hush falls over the arena.
DANNY	Hurry up.

ANGELO	Face off!
DANNY	Lemieux takes the puck.
ANGELO	Intercepted by Sundin…
DANNY	But he loses it. Lemieux is moving fast.
ANGELO	But not fast enough. Sundin passes to Amazing Angelo. Angelo across the blue lines. Angelo on the breakaway.
PENELOPE	*(waving her arms in the air)* STOP!
ANGELO	*(startled)* What?
PENELOPE	I don't want to play anymore.
ANGELO	I don't believe it.
PENELOPE	Let's play something else.
ANGELO	I would have scored. I would have won.
PENELOPE	Okay, you score, you win. Woo-woo. Let's do something else. I'll be the star.

> *They notice DANNY limping, putting his boots back on.*

PENELOPE	Hey, are you okay?
ANGELO	Your feet must be so cold.
PENELOPE	Of course they're cold. They're freezing.
DANNY	They're okay.
PENELOPE	Why do you wear those boots? They're so old fashioned.
DANNY	They're okay.
PENELOPE	I wouldn't wear them if you paid me.
DANNY	They're okay. Okay?
ANGELO	Yeah, who cares.

> *Beat.*

PENELOPE	I think I've been nice long enough.

> *She turns and leaves.*

DANNY	Okay, but it's your turn.

PENELOPE   My turn for what?

DANNY   To choose a game.

PENELOPE   Excuse me. I think I'm a little too mature for games.

ANGELO   So let's play hockey!

PENELOPE   You just wanna score.

ANGELO   I like scoring.

PENELOPE   Too bad you can't score on the ice.

ANGELO   Shut up!

ANGELO walks away.

DANNY   Why can't you score?

ANGELO   I can. Sometimes. I mean I get a breakaway, right, I go to shoot and then this thought comes into my head that says, "YOU'RE GOING TO BLOW IT, YOU'RE GOING TO BLOW IT" and I blow it.

PENELOPE   That's a brain freeze.

ANGELO   A brain freeze?

PENELOPE   I get them all the time in ballet. I'm trying to do Grand Jette and Madam says VITE! VITE! VITE! And I get so freaked I jump like a frog.

DANNY   So Anj. You got a bad thought in your head. Want me to get it out?

ANGELO   Yeah right.

DANNY   I can if you let me.

ANGELO   You can?

DANNY   Uh-huh.

ANGELO   How?

DANNY   Sit down Mr. Angelo. Nurse, get me the knife.

PENELOPE   My mother doesn't let me take knives outside.

DANNY   Not a real knife. A game knife, 'cause we gotta open up his head.

ANGELO	What?
PENELOPE	Okay.
ANGELO	Not okay.
PENELOPE	Only I get to be the doctor.
ANGELO	No.
PENELOPE	It's my turn so it's my game. Besides I know what doctors do. I've got the operation station.
DANNY	Doctor. Your knife.
PENELOPE	I don't need a knife. I need a saw.
ANGELO	I gotta go.
DANNY	Sit down, sir. This won't hurt a bit. It'll hurt a lot.

> *Horror laugh. DANNY mimes giving an injection using props from his cart and providing sound effects. PENELOPE noisily saws across ANGELO's forehead using a hockey stick, and pries open his head. DANNY wraps ANGELO's head in a scarf and they stare inside.*

PENELOPE	Hmmmm…
DANNY	Aaaaaa…
ANGELO	What?
PENELOPE	There's no brain. Magnifying glass. *(She looks.)* There it is.
DANNY	A brain freeze.
PENELOPE	And it's growing! Get the blow torch.
ANGELO	Blow torch?
DANNY	Just relax, sir. It only hurts if your head melts.
PENELOPE	Stand back–

> *Cell phone rings. PENELOPE answers both phones.*

> Yes…. Oh hi Dad. *(She walks away.)* Listen don't get mad okay…. Promise?… Mom doesn't believe you put the

cheque in the mail…. Daddy, please don't call her that…. Can't you tell her?… Okay…. Okay…

DANNY   *(warning)* Doctor… he's bleeding.

PENELOPE   Daddy look. My patient's head is wide open. I have to go.

She hangs up.

All right. I'm back.

ANGELO   Oh yay.

DANNY   If you feel something burning, relax, it's all part of the process.

PENELOPE   *Hasta la vista*, freezy. *(She torches ANGELO's brain.)* Hey. It disappeared.

DANNY   Where'd it go?

ANGELO   You know. I'm feeling a lot better.

DANNY   Doctor. It's gone to his stomach.

PENELOPE   Start laser cutters. We're going in.

ANGELO   Aaaaaaah…

DANNY and PENELOPE cut ANGELO open.

PENELOPE   Ew. Does he need these things?

DANNY   I don't think so. What about this?

PENELOPE   That's his heart.

ANGELO   Put it back.

DANNY   It stopped.

PENELOPE   It stopped?

ANGELO   It stopped?

PENELOPE   Emergency. Get the demib, de-rib, ah heck, get me the "stand clear" thingy!

DANNY   Charged and ready, Doctor.

PENELOPE   Stand clear. Bumf. Clear. Bumf. Clear.

DANNY   Wait. The heart is beating.

PENELOPE   And the brain… it's thinking!

ANGELO   Isn't it time for a commercial?

PENELOPE   Not quite. We still haven't found the bad thought. Nurse, get me the Thought Identifier Kit – stat.

DANNY   Right here Doctor.

PENELOPE   Hmmm. There are so many. Can you describe the bad one?

ANGELO   Describe a thought?!

DANNY   Quick! Time is running out.

               DANNY makes a ticking sound.

ANGELO   Well… it's loud and it jumps into my head when I'm not looking and it's really scary and it… it… sounds like my dad.

PENELOPE   Got it!

               PENELOPE pulls a wriggling, red scarf out of ANGELO's head.

DANNY   It's still alive.

PENELOPE   Get it.

ANGELO   Stomp on it.

ALL   *(stomping)* Aaaaaaaaah!

PENELOPE   It's dead.

DANNY   It's gone.

ANGELO   Guys. It's a scarf.

DANNY   But your brain freeze is gone.

PENELOPE   You're going to score!

ANGELO   Look, I know you want to help, but you can't fix anything with a game.

DANNY   Yes you can. If you believe it.

ANGELO   Yeah, well I guess that's the problem… I don't believe it.

               The dinosaur roars off.

	I gotta go.
DANNY	Wait. I'm going to talk with your dad.
ANGELO	What?
PENELOPE	No.
ANGELO	You can't.
DANNY	Why not?
ANGELO	He doesn't like kids.
DANNY	I'll use a disguise.
ANGELO	He sees through disguises.
PENELOPE	And he reads your thoughts.
ANGELO	And if he doesn't like them–
PENELOPE	He eats you alive.
DANNY	*(He looks at them then walks over to his walkie-talkie.)* Control? It's Delco. I gotta Code Red with a dinosaur, and I'm going in.

He walks toward the door.

PENELOPE	Danny…
ANGELO	Please…
PENELOPE	It's not a game.
DANNY	Of course it's a game. Everything's a game. But if I don't come back, stay friends, okay?

DANNY opens the door.

Hello…?

Dinosaur rumble. DANNY exits.

ANGELO	I can't believe he's going to talk to my dad. No one talks to my dad.
PENELOPE	I can't even look at your dad.
ANGELO	Sometimes… neither can I.

Beat.

PENELOPE	Angelo? *(beat)* Are we friends? *(beat)* It's just… Danny said we should stay friends.
ANGELO	We're not friends, Penny.
PENELOPE	We used to be. *(beat)* And then you started playing hockey and I went to a different school. We met different people and we just drifted apart.
ANGELO	You treated me like an empty chip bag.
PENELOPE	I did not.
ANGELO	You treated me like a dead battery.
PENELOPE	I did not.
ANGELO	You said I had to be your slave for life.
PENELOPE	Okay, so maybe I did say that.
ANGELO	You think it's funny.
PENELOPE	Okay, I'm sorry.
ANGELO	As if you mean it.
PENELOPE	I do mean it. I do. I'm sorry. Really.

Cell phone rings.

Hello?… Hi Mom…. Yes he called…. He said "the stupid cheque is in the stupid mail…." Well that's what he said…. Mom…. I know but…. Why can't you…. Okay! Sheesh.

Other cell phone rings.

Hold on. *(switches)* Hello?… Oh hi Dad. Guess what? Mom's on the other phone…. Yes I told her…. Okay, but you got to promise you won't get angry…. Then I'm not going to tell you…. Okay, Mom wants you to bring the money over in cash…. Dad, you promised!… *(gasps)* That is such a bad word. *(switches)* Mom, Dad says it's a little inconvenient right now…. Mom…. Please…. *(switches)* Dad, Mom is feeling a little frustrated…. I don't know who's fault it is…. No excuse me I don't know. *(both)* I don't know, I don't know. I'm just a kid. Talk to each other.

PENELOPE jams the two cell phones together and helplessly holds them out in front of her. ANGELO grabs his scarf and ties the phones together. He opens the garbage can and motions for her to drop them inside. She does. The garbage can shakes a little, and then stops.

Wow. I put my parents in a garbage can. *(smiling)* I'm going to be in so much trouble.

DANNY enters eating a sandwich.

DANNY   Hi guys.

PENELOPE   Danny! You're alive!

DANNY   Yup.

PENELOPE   Did he crush you in his jaws? Did he rip out your heart?

DANNY   Naw.

ANGELO   He didn't even yell?

DANNY   At first, yeah, but then I told him about my super coat and how I'd moved eight times in two years and he made me a salami sandwich. Hey. Why is your dad at home?

ANGELO   He lost his job.

DANNY   Oh.

ANGELO   And now my mom works two jobs.

DANNY   That explains everything. See, when adults have a job, they disguise themselves as workers and they don't have time for anything. But when they don't have a job, they have lots of time which should be good, right? But actually it turns them into dinosaurs and they bite your head off. *(The others look confused.)* It's an adult problem.

FATHER   *(off)* Angelo. Lunchtime.

ANGELO   Wow!

PENELOPE   It's your dad.

ANGELO   Coming. *(at his door)* But what if the dinosaur comes back.

DANNY	It will, but now you know it's just your dad in disguise.
ANGELO	Cool! See ya later.

> *ANGELO exits. The garbage can rattles.*

DANNY	What's that?
PENELOPE	My parents.
DANNY	Are you going to let them out?
PENELOPE	They need to talk. Have you really moved eight times in two years?
DANNY	Yup.
PENELOPE	I've always lived right here.
DANNY	You'll get to move someday.
PENELOPE	I hope you don't move for a looooooong time.
DANNY	Don't count on it.
PENELOPE	Why not?
DANNY	I gotta get to the mountains, remember?
PENELOPE	Oh. Right.

> *The garbage can shakes. PENELOPE goes to retrieve the phones.*

I guess I better take them out. *(She does.)* So…. Thanks! I mean…. See ya.

> *She exits.*

DANNY	Control? Delco. Situation normal. Strangely normal. No explosions, no sneak attacks. Something's wrong. Something always goes wrong.

> *LOUISE enters.*

LOUISE	Danny?
DANNY	Hi.
LOUISE	Who are you talking to?
DANNY	Control.

LOUISE	*(proudly)* I'm home from work.
DANNY	Did you get paid?
LOUISE	Cash on the barrel. *(DANNY puts out his hand.)* I'm going to be the banker now.
DANNY	Mom.
LOUISE	I can handle it.
DANNY	We made a deal.
LOUISE	That was before. I can handle it now.
DANNY	We'll get kicked out.
LOUISE	No we won't.
DANNY	We always do when you keep the money.
LOUISE	Not always.
DANNY	You spend it.
LOUISE	Not always.
DANNY	So where is it? *(beat)* Show me.
LOUISE	Okay. I spent it.
DANNY	See?
LOUISE	But I spent it on you.
DANNY	It's always the same.
LOUISE	On boots. You need some new boots.
DANNY	My boots are fine.
LOUISE	They're too big. Look. These are just your size.
DANNY	Take them back.
LOUISE	I can't.
DANNY	Why not?
LOUISE	They were on sale.
DANNY	Stupid, stupid, stupid, stupid–
LOUISE	Danny calm down.

DANNY	That's okay. I like moving.
LOUISE	Danny…
DANNY	I'm the king of moving.
LOUISE	Things are looking good for us. I've got a job. You've got friends. Look at me. *(He does.)* We're not moving.
DANNY	Does Dad know we're here?
LOUISE	No.
DANNY	How come he never writes us?
LOUISE	Cutting trees must keep him busy.
DANNY	I thought he fought fires.
LOUISE	Danny, there's something I have to tell you about your dad.
DANNY	No. I'm going to try on these boots.
LOUISE	Danny–
DANNY	They look brand new second hand.
LOUISE	Listen to me.
DANNY	I'll be able to run like the wind in these.

He takes off his boots.

LOUISE	Danny! What happened to your feet.
DANNY	Nothing.
LOUISE	They're bleeding.
DANNY	I was playing hockey.
LOUISE	In your socks?
DANNY	My boots were too big.
LOUISE	Why didn't you wear your running shoes?
DANNY	I don't have any running shoes.
LOUISE	Of course you do. I bought some for you. Didn't I? Didn't I?! Ohmigod. Is that why you skip gym class? Is it? How

long…? How long have you been…. How long have you been with no shoes?

DANNY   C'mon, Mom. It doesn't matter. It doesn't matter.

> *DANNY leads his mother off to their apartment.*

ACT THREE

Time passes. Clinton street turns into a school playground. We hear the voices of other children in the background.

DANNY and ANGELO are standing in the playground before school. DANNY is eating from ANGELO's lunch bag. PENELOPE sneaks up on them.

PENELOPE Hi! What are you doing?

DANNY Having breakfast.

ANGELO My dad packed a double lunch.

PENELOPE My mom packed a double lunch too.

DANNY *(mouth full)* That's okay. I'll eat both.

ANGELO What are you doing over here anyway? This is the boys' corner.

PENELOPE I want to know what we're playing after school.

DANNY I've got new orders from Control.

PENELOPE I bet they want us to make a big budget movie with me as star.

ANGELO Yeah, right.

PENELOPE *(teasing)* You can be my lover.

ANGELO Gag.

PENELOPE All right, you can be my limo driver.

ANGELO Deal.

PENELOPE Danny can be my lover. *(gasps)*

A gaggle of giggling girls passes on and off. PENELOPE hides behind the boys.

ANGELO Why are you hiding?

PENELOPE I'm in disguise. So what's the game?

DANNY The game is – escape!

ANGELO	From who?
DANNY	The Scarlet Hand.
PENELOPE	No. The Scarlet Hand of Evil.
ANGELO	No. The Scarlet Hand of the mutant Martian snake monkeys.

They crack up. PENELOPE's phone rings.

PENELOPE	Hello?… Sure. *(She hands the phone to DANNY.)* It's for you.
DANNY	Hello?

LOUISE steps forward with a phone.

LOUISE	Hi honey.
DANNY	Hi.
LOUISE	Aw, ya just won't believe it, eh? Ya just won't believe it.
DANNY	What?
LOUISE	Things were going so good, so smooth I thought just for once…
DANNY	*(He moves away.)* What's wrong?
LOUISE	It's Old Joe. He's in the hospital. They took him this morning in an ambulance.
DANNY	Is he okay?
LOUISE	I dunno.
DANNY	What about your job?
LOUISE	The sandwich shop is closed. Who knows for how long? Look I might be late getting home, okay? I gotta figure out what's going on.
DANNY	Is it moving time?
LOUISE	I dunno. Maybe. Who knows.
DANNY	Mom…?
LOUISE	It was looking so good, so good.
DANNY	It's okay, Mom. I like moving. I'm the King of Moving.

LOUISE   You're the King of Hearts, buddy. The King of flamin' Hearts.

She leaves.

DANNY   Mom? Mom?

PENELOPE   Is everything okay?

DANNY   Yeah. Everything's fine.

School bell. A classroom rolls forward.

PRINCIPAL   *(voiceover)* Just two announcements this morning. First a reminder that raffle tickets for the gingerbread house are still available at the school office. This raffle is for sports equipment and is not to be confused with last week's raffle for library books. And congratulations to our girls volleyball team for almost winning their game yesterday afternoon. Have a good day everyone and remember – work smart, work hard AND work together.

PENELOPE waves her hand, is chosen, stands and reads easily.

PENELOPE   "'Never laugh at live dragons, Bilbo you fool!' he said to himself, and it became a favourite saying of his later, and passed into a proverb. 'You aren't nearly through this adventure yet.'"

PENELOPE looks up to an imaginary teacher and sits down disappointed. ANGELO stands and reads.

ANGELO   "The dragon spooted–

PENELOPE   Spouted.

ANGELO   Spouted terrific flames after him, and fast through–

PENELOPE   Though.

ANGELO   Fast though he sped up the slope, he was nearly overcome and stumbled blin-dly–

PENELOPE   Blindly.

ANGELO   Blindly on in great pain and fear."

ANGELO sits relieved. PENELOPE wants to read again, but it's DANNY who is chosen.

DANNY   But then Bilbo got angry at the dragon and throwing off
               his disguise took out his sword which sent light flashing
               everywhere and he jumped on the dragon's back and
               started climbing towards its fiery head, climbing and
               climbing, stabbing and stabbing while the dragon
               smashed his head into the walls and… *(He looks up.)*
               No. It's not what's written. It's better. *(ANGELO and*
               PENELOPE giggle.) …I can't read it if it's boring. There
               should be a part for mutant Martian snake monkeys.
               (PENELOPE, ANGELO and DANNY giggle and then stop
               suddenly.) …Sure I'd be happy to read for the principal.

               DANNY leaves.

PENELOPE   Please, Miss. May I go to the washroom?

               PENELOPE leaves.

ANGELO   Please Miss. May I go to the washroom?… Oh please.
               I really gotta go. Really really really really gotta gotta
               gotta gotta – thanks.

               ANGELO exits.

               DANNY enters down a corridor. PENELOPE and
               ANGELO enter following him.

PENELOPE   Danny.

DANNY   What?

PENELOPE   The principal's office is down there.

DANNY   I'm not going.

ANGELO   You have to.

PENELOPE   You're going to get in so much trouble.

DANNY   Who cares? My mom lost her job. This school is history.
               (beat) You guys don't get it, do you. No job, no money.
               No money, no rent. No rent and it's moving time.

ANGELO   My dad lost his job. We didn't move.

PENELOPE   My mom will give you the money. She knows you're
               poor.

DANNY	I'm not poor. Look. What's the big deal. It was going to happen eventually.
ANGELO	But it's not supposed to happen. People are supposed to stay in one place. They're supposed to go to school and have friends.
PENELOPE	I don't want you to go.
DANNY	C'mon. Don't drop your disguise. It's a game.
PENELOPE	Moving's not a game. Moving's for real.
DANNY	This always happens. You make a game, you have fun and then someone *always* has to break it. I'm moving. You think I want to stay in a lousy basement apartment all my life?
PENELOPE	It's not that bad.
DANNY	How would you know, Penny? How would you know what it's like to be me. You don't know anything.
PENELOPE	I know you can't read.
DANNY	That's a lie.
PENELOPE	In class. You make up stories 'cause you don't know how to read.
	Pause.
DANNY	Who else knows?
ANGELO	I do.
PENELOPE	Everyone knows.
DANNY	You guys are such losers. Both of you. But hey. Good news. I'll never have to see either of you again.
	DANNY runs. Clinton Street re-appears. DANNY dashes up to his door just as LOUISE enters. She comes up to him.
LOUISE	Danny. Why aren't you at school?
DANNY	Came back to pack. Are we going to a shelter?
LOUISE	No.

DANNY	Aw, c'mon. The food is bad but the TV is great. I'll be packed in a flash.
LOUISE	Danny, we're not going anywhere.
DANNY	It's okay, Mom. I know. You lost your job.
LOUISE	I thought I'd lost my job. Oh honey, listen. I went to the hospital. Old Joe is sick but until he gets better he wants me to be the manager. Maybe forever. Six hundred a week plus tips. We're home sweet home.
DANNY	This isn't my home. I want to move.
LOUISE	I thought you were having fun, making friends…
DANNY	They're just pretend friends.
LOUISE	Aw, don't say that.
DANNY	I want to be with Dad.
LOUISE	Let's go inside and talk about it.
DANNY	I'm never going in that place again. I'm going to the Rockies. Now.
LOUISE	Your dad doesn't live in the Rockies. He's never lived in the Rockies. I don't know where he lives.
DANNY	What?
LOUISE	It was a story, honey, a story so we could have something… something bright… something clean–
DANNY	You're lying.
LOUISE	Truth, Danny. True blue.
DANNY	You're lying so I won't leave. So I won't leave you and find Dad.
LOUISE	Oh Danny…
DANNY	You're jealous 'cause he's in the mountains and you're in a lousy basement.
LOUISE	There's nothing wrong with where we live.
DANNY	Except for one thing, Louise.
LOUISE	Okay. Come on inside.

DANNY	Gonna make me?
LOUISE	Look. I know you're upset–
DANNY	No. I'm happy. I'm happy 'cause I'm leaving you.
LOUISE	You're not leaving.
DANNY	No more razzle dazzle. No more stupid jokes. No more lies.
LOUISE	Danny, please…
DANNY	Aw. Have I upset you?
LOUISE	All right, mister. We're going inside, right now. Right now, do you hear?
DANNY	Nice disguise Mom. Too bad its too late.
LOUISE	Danny! Danny! Come back here!

DANNY runs off.

Music underneath.

PENELOPE	*(on the phone)* Anj.
ANGELO	*(on the phone)* Hey.
PENELOPE	Have you see Danny?
ANGELO	No.
PENELOPE	He's gone.
ANGELO	What?
PENELOPE	He's run away from home.
ANGELO	C'mon.
PENELOPE	His mother's called the police.
LOUISE	*(on the phone)* I'd like to report a runaway child.
PENELOPE	She wants us to help.
LOUISE	His name is Danny Carter.
ANGELO	I'll check the park.
PENELOPE	I'll check the schoolyard.

ANGELO	I'll check Bloor Street.
PENELOPE	I'll check College.
LOUISE	I'm his mother…. He doesn't have any other family.
ANGELO	Cliff? Hey. Have you seen Danny?
PENELOPE	Stace? Hey. Have you seen Danny?
ANGELO	Peter?
PENELOPE	Anjelija?
ANGELO	José?
PENELOPE	Tessa?
ANGELO & PENELOPE	Have you seen Danny?
LOUISE	No, I don't know where he went. That's why I'm calling you…. He was wearing a plaid shirt and blue jeans…. He's just a little boy. You have to find him.
PENELOPE	Anj?
ANGELO	Hey.
PENELOPE	Did you find him?
ANGELO	No. Louise?
LOUISE	Yes?
ANGELO	Did you find him?
LOUISE	No. Penelope?
PENELOPE	Yes?
LOUISE	Did you find him?
PENELOPE	No.
LOUISE	What time is it?
PENELOPE	Ten o'clock. What time is it?
ANGELO	Twelve o'clock. What time is it?
LOUISE	Ohmigod. It's three in the morning. Danny.

LOUISE, PENELOPE and ANGELO exit.

**RADIO
BROADCAST** *(voiceover)* And in weather tonight, we have a frost warning for the Metro area. Temperatures will plunge well below zero as a result of a severe low pressure system moving in from the North-West…

DANNY pushes a hospital bed centre stage.

LOUISE *(off, as if she is walking, calling)* Danny… Danny… Danny…

DANNY ceremoniously tosses a sheet into the air. We hear a heart monitor beating.

A DOCTOR and a NURSE in masks enter. Their backs to the audience concealing the bed, they begin working. DANNY watches. LOUISE paces.

DOCTOR What's his core temperature?

NURSE Thirty-two.

DOCTOR Let's re-warm him.

DANNY Wow. Real doctors… real nurses… and they're trying to save me.

NURSE His heart is brachycardic.

DOCTOR Let's intubate and stand by with oxygen.

Heart begins to speed up.

DANNY I was trying to get to the mountains to see my dad. I took the subway Christie, Ossington, Dufferin, Landsdowne all the way to Kipling and started walking West. It was raining and then the rain started freezing and I was going to the mountains to see my dad but my dad doesn't live there anymore. My dad never lived there.

NURSE Patient at risk of V-Tach, Doctor.

DOCTOR I can hear it. Get me 10cc's of noradrenaline.

DANNY I crawled under a bridge and I was really cold but I had my super-coat and I guess I went to sleep 'cause it was morning when they found me. Well, actually it was a dog that found me. I remember its breath was hot on my face and it licked my ear. That's when I tried to wake up but I couldn't. I guess I wasn't really sleeping. I guess I wasn't breathing much either.

> *The heart is now very fast and shallow, and then it stops.*

NURSE   No heartbeat.

DOCTOR   Get the defibulator.

DANNY   It's nice they're trying to save me but I dunno…

NURSE   Charging.

DANNY   If I can't go to the mountains I'm not going back.

NURSE   Ready.

DOCTOR   Clear.

> *Sound of defibulator.*

NURSE   No response.

DANNY   Back to that school, back to those kids, back to that basement–

LOUISE   Danny.

DANNY   Back to my mom.

LOUISE   Come on Danny.

DANNY   Mom?

LOUISE   Please Danny. Ohmigod. Please.

DANNY   You'd be really sad if I left, and you'd get lost on the subway and spend all your money and if I left, you wouldn't be a mother and I know that's what you really want to be.

NURSE   Ready.

DOCTOR   Clear.

> *Sound of defibulator.*

DANNY   Maybe I should–

NURSE   We've got something.

DANNY   Maybe I should stay.

Heart begins.

EPILOGUE

Hospital room.

DANNY is looking at an atlas.

LOUISE enters.

LOUISE	Hey.
DANNY	Hey.
LOUISE	You reading a book?
DANNY	It's a map book. I thought the Rockies were on the other side of Mississauga.
LOUISE	How ya feeling?
DANNY	Okay. My toes still hurt, but who's counting.
LOUISE	I am. The doctor says you can go home.
DANNY	Oh.
LOUISE	What's home to you, Danny?
DANNY	I dunno.
LOUISE	I do. Home is 92B for basement Clinton Street.
DANNY	Okay.
LOUISE	I'm sorry I lied about your dad.
DANNY	I kinda guessed. I'm just sad.
LOUISE	You have every right to be sad.
DANNY	Not me. I'm sad for him. He missed all the fun of being with us.
LOUISE	You're amazing.
DANNY	No you're amazing.
LOUISE	No you're amazing.
DANNY	All right, I'm amazing.
LOUISE	You look well enough to come home right now.
DANNY	No, Mom, please. They got cable here and the Movie Channel…

LOUISE	Angelo and Penelope are here.
DANNY	I don't want to see them.
LOUISE	They're your friends, Danny. They've been coming over every day asking how you are. Just say hello.

ANGELO and PENELOPE enter.

ANGELO	Hey.
PENELOPE	Hey.

Embarrassed silence.

LOUISE	I'll be right outside.

LOUISE exits.

ANGELO	So…
DANNY	So…
PENELOPE	So is it true you almost died cause you were frozen and they had to stick things down your throat and now you have to pee in a bag?
DANNY	They're saying I'm either really lucky or really stupid.
PENELOPE	Anj's got something to show you.
ANGELO	It's nothing much…
DANNY	A puck?
ANGELO	Yeah. It's my first goal. My dad wrote the date on it.
DANNY	Cool.
PENELOPE	And I got you a present.

He passes him an envelope.

DANNY	Thanks. What does it say?
PENELOPE	It's a gift certificate to the Gap.
DANNY	Cool.
PENELOPE	No offense but you really need it.
DANNY	So what you guys been doing?
ANGELO	Nothing.

PENELOPE	It's so boring.
ANGELO	When are you coming home?
DANNY	I dunno…
ANGELO	Don't you want to?
DANNY	Oh yeah, you guys are good it's just… the school thing.
ANGELO	What about it?
DANNY	Well I get into class and I look at the words and this thought comes into my head. YOU'LL NEVER READ. YOU'LL NEVER READ. Why are you looking at me like that?
PENELOPE	Nurse, get me a saw.
DANNY	Oh wait a minute.
ANGELO	Electric saw or chain saw.
PENELOPE	All the saws. We're going to take that bad thought OUT!

Music.

The end.

David S. Craig was the founding Artistic Director of Theatre Direct Canada and is currently the Artistic Director of Roseneath Theatre. He has written more than twenty professionally produced plays including *Fires in the Night* for the Blyth Festival, *Booster McCrane, P.M.* for Toronto Free Theatre, *Cue for Treason* for Young People's Theatre and his one-man show *Napalm the Magnificent* for Roseneath Theatre. With Robert Morgan he has written *Morgan's Journey, Head à Tête, The Book of Miracles, Health Class* and *Dib and Dob and the Journey Home*. For CBC Radio, David created a fifty-one part series for Morningside based on *Booster McCrane, P.M.* and for Metro Morning, a fifty-minute series titled "Diamond Lane."